THE AUTHOR

Pierluigi Romeo di Colloredo Mels was born in Rome in 1966. Archaeologist and military historian, he is the author of numerous works on the history of the two world wars and the Italian interwar conflicts, Ethiopia and Spain, and of the units of the MVSN, the subject of which he is considered one of the leading international experts. Among his latest works, *Camicia Nera! Storia delle unità combattenti della Milizia Volontaria Sicurezza Nazionale dalle origini al 25 luglio, Südfront. Il Feldmaresciallo Albert Kesselring nella campagna d'Italia 1943- 1945; Da Sidi el Barrani a Beda Fomm 1940- 1941; Per vincere ci vogliono i leoni… I fronti dimenticati delle camicie nere, 1939- 1940; Controguerriglia! La 2a Armata italiana e l'occupazione dei Balcani 1941- 1943; Confine orientale. Italiani e slavi sull'Amarissimo dal Risorgimento all'esodo; Giugno 1940. La battaglia delle Alpi*. Colloredo is also editor of Storia Rivista and collaborates with the magazines Nova Historica, Storia in Rete, Ritterkreuz, Fronti di guerra and Il Primato Nazionale.

PUBLISHING'S NOTES

None of unpublished images or text of our book may be reproduced in any format without the expressed written permission of Luca Cristini Editore (already Soldiershop.com) when not indicate as marked with license creative commons 3.0 or 4.0. Luca Cristini Editore has made every reasonable effort to locate, contact and acknowledge rights holders and to correctly apply terms and conditions to Content.
Every effort has been made to trace the copyright of all the photographs. If there are unintentional omissions, please contact the publisher in writing at: info@soldiershop.com, who will correct all subsequent editions.
Our trademark: Luca Cristini Editore@, and the names of our series & brand: Soldiershop, Witness to war, Museum book, Bookmoon, Soldiers&Weapons, Battlefield, War in colour, Historical Biographies, Darwin's view, Fabula, Altrastoria, Italia Storica Ebook, Witness To History, Soldiers, Weapons & Uniforms, Storia etc. are herein @ by Luca Cristini Editore.

LICENSES COMMONS

This book may utilize part of material marked with license creative commons 3.0 or 4.0 (CC BY 4.0), (CC BY-ND 4.0), (CC BY-SA 4.0) or (CC0 1.0). We give appropriate attribution credit and indicate if change were made in the acknowledgments field. Our WTW books series utilize only fonts licensed under the SIL Open Font License or other free use license.

For a complete list of Soldiershop titles please contact Luca Cristini Editore on our website: www.soldiershop.com or www.cristinieditore.com.
E-mail: info@soldiershop.com

Title: **ITALIAN BLACK SHIRTS ON EASTERN FRONT 1941- 1943 CODE.: WTW-017 EN** by Pierluigi Romeo di Colloredo Mels.
ISBN code: 978-88-93276450 First edition: september 2020 (ebook ISBN 97888932766467)
Language: English Nr. of images: 119 dimensions: 177,8x254mm Cover & Art Design: Luca S. Cristini

WITNESS TO WAR (SOLDIERSHOP) is a trademark of Luca Cristini Editore, via Orio, 35/4 - 24050 Zanica (BG) ITALY.

WITNESS TO WAR

ITALIAN BLACK SHIRTS ON THE EASTERN FRONT 1941- 1943

PHOTOS & IMAGES FROM WORLD WARTIME ARCHIVES

PIERLUIGI ROMEO DI COLLOREDO MELS

BOOKS TO COLLECT

SUMMARY

The operations of the 63rd Tagliamento CCNN Assault Legion in 1941..........................Pag. 5

The Christmas battle (December 1941)..Pag. 21

The *Raggruppamento 3 Gennaio* and the First defensive battle of the Don (August 1942)...Pag. 43

The Second defensive battle of the Don and the withdraval, December '42-January '43......Pag. 65

The M.V.S.N. Croatian Legion. *(Hrvatske Legija)*..Pag. 85

Bibliography..Pag. 98

▲ The Black Shirts of the Tagliamento Legion leaving for the Russian front, 1941.

On September 9th, 1941, the *Tagliamento*'s Black Shirts replaced the Lancieri di Novara Regiment in protection of a stretch of the western bank of the Dnjepr near Dnjeprodsershink, being employed by the 3rd *Celere Amedeo Duca d'Aosta* Division.

On the banks of the Dnjepr the legionaries had the baptism of fire, repelling three Soviet assaults, and losing in these first fights twelve fallen and eighteen wounded.

On the 21st the *Tagliamento* left the right bank of the river, and alongside the *Torino* Division supported the actions of the infantrymen and the SS of the Regiments 9. Germania and 10 Westland of the 5. SS *Panzerdivision Wiking* of the Gruppenführer Felix Steiner, in the bridgehead of Dnjepropetrowsk. The *Torino* Division and the *Tagliamento* Legion (strengthened by the 2nd anti-tank battalion) on one side, and the *Pasubio* on the other, each moving towards the other, respectively from the bridgehead of Dnjepropetrowsk and from the positions conquered by the infantrymen of the 79th *Roma* of the *Pasubio* div. on 'Orely river should have closed in a bag, with no escape, all the Soviet units present in the loop of the Dnjepr.

The Black Shirts were chosen not only for the combativeness but also for the mobility superior to that of the normal infantry. The legionaries were able to march more quickly, because, despite being equipped with an insufficient number of vehicles to transport men, backpacks and equipment were loaded on the trucks, with the exception of individual armament, allowing the soldiers to march lighter and therefore faster, what provoked the envy of the infantry, forced to march completely hurrying: the infantrymen who arrived in Russia invariably "had it" with the CC.NN. The latter also walked, proceeding boldly with the horse of St. Francis, [ie by feet] but they went faster because they had no impedimenia; all baggage was trucked. The poor infantrymen, on the other hand, nothing: the packed backpack, the rifle, the gas mask, the hand grenades, the magazines and whoever has more.

The action took place in three stages, on September 28, 29 and 30. The *Torino* Division and the 63rd Legion moved forward at half past seven in the morning, after a short and violent artillery fire, overcoming with impetus and great cooperation between infantrymen and legionaries (as Messe himself recognized) both the numerous minefields and the tenacious defense of the riflemen of the 261st Soviet Division.

▲ Mussolini inspects the departments of the Legion CC.NN. Tagliamento before leaving for Russia. From left Lieutenant Commander of the Legion, Consul General Niccolò Nicchiarelli and the Head of State.

THE OPERATIONS OF THE 63ᴿᴰ TAGLIAMENTO CCNN ASSAULT LEGION IN 1941

The 63rd *Tagliamento* Assault Legion was formed in February 1941 with the Black Shirts battalions LXIII ° of Udine (under the command of Primo Seniore Ermacora Zuliani) and LXXIX ° - coming from the *Tagliamento* legion - of Reggio Emilia (Primo Seniore Patroncini) and with the 183rd gunner company of Piacenza (cent. A. Zanotti). The command was entrusted to the Lieutenant General Niccolò Nicchiarelli. The troops were placed under the command of the 63rd *Tagliamento* Legion, which had its headquarters in Udine in peacetime, and, as mentioned, the Emilians of the LXXIX ° battalion and the machine-gunners of the 183rd company were added to the Friulians of the Zuliani battalion; however the firepower was still less than needed for a front use. Therefore, when the 63rd was later transformed into a truck-mounted Legion, an additional machine-gun company was assigned to it, the 103rd company CC.NN[1]. of Cuneo (commanded by the *Tagliamento*[2] M. Gentile), and a battalion of the Royal Army (LXIII ° Weapons battalion *Sassari*) in order to increase its firepower.

With the beginning of Operation Barbarossa and Mussolini's decision to send an Italian contingent to the USSR, the Legion *Tagliamento* was chosen to represent the Fascist *Milizia Volontaria per la Sicurezza Nazionale*[3]: it was made up of 1191 officers and black shirts, and 284 officers and soldiers of the Royal Army belonging to the LXIII ° battalion AA, mobilized by the deposit of the 151st *Sassari* Infantry Regiment, under the command of Lieutenant Colonel V. De Franco; to the Royal Army belonged also the 133 drivers employed to the vehicles of the Legion. The *Tagliamento* was therefore to represent the Black Shirts and the National Fascist Party in the crusade against Soviet communism, alongside the large army units.

Between 9th and 10th August the *Tagliamento* Legion, transported by five trains, crossed the Brenner border reaching Trusesti, Romania, from where, on the 23rd of the same month, it moved by ordinary way to Perwomajsk.

Here arrived the 63rd Legion was placed, on 27th August, under the operational dependencies of the *Torino* Transportable Infantry Division (81st and 82nd Infantry Rgts); the following day, at the crossroads of Ladishinka, eighteen kilometers south of Uman, the Legion, together with other units, was reviewed by Mussolini, Hitler, accompanied by their respective General Staff, and by General Giovanni Messe, commander of the Corps of Italian expedition to Russia. This is how Dino Alfieri described the scene:

"Due to the truly disastrous ground conditions of the ground [the rewiew] took place so that it was inevitably a little messy. The drivers of the trucks made efforts to keep their distance, to proceed on the same line, to reduce slippage. The departments were well presented, the soldiers were shaved, the weapons well kept. When they passed in front of Mussolini, and turned their faces towards him with a jerk, many were unable to hold back an expression of complacency and contentment".

---

[1] CCNN: *Camicie Nere*, Black Shirts
[2] Captain. The Fascist Militia used ranks inspired by the *Roman* ones (a.e. *Console* for Colonel, *Seniore* for Major, *Capomanipolo* for Leutenant, etc.)
[3] MVSN, *National Volounteer Militia for National Security*, the Fascist Militia, i.e. Black Shirts, the fourth Italian Armed Force, alongside Army, Navy and Airforce, also used for internal security. Cfr P. Battistelli, P. Cruciani, Italian Black Shirts 1935-1945, Oxford 2010.

At sixteen the Italian troops had reached the targets set on the Obuskowskije-Goranowskije line, inflicting numerous losses on the enemy and capturing materials and weapons.

The following day, on the 29th, the second part of the maneuver took place, the advance on Petrikowka: *Tagliamento* and the *Torino* Division would have advanced to the Kurilowka-Petrikowka line on two columns, the right one formed by the *Tagliamento* together with the 81st Regiment; at the same time the *Pasubio* Division, (to which were aggregated for the occasion an Italian motorcycle company, the 2nd Squadron of the Light tanks Group San Giorgio and the German kampfgruppe Abraham) would have moved south from the bridgehead of Zaritschanka on the Orely river until to reach the Galushkowka-Petrikowka line.

At 5.30 in the morning the right column of the *Torino* battlegroup (*Tagliamento* and 81st infantry); the avant-garde Black Shirts, flanked by the infantrymen of the 3rd battalion of the 81st *Torino* Infantry Regiment, reached the village of Petrikowka at eighteen joining the *Pasubio* and closing the bag. In these actions, until 30 September, in the face of very slight losses (two fallen and fourteen injured), the *Tagliamento* had captured 646 Soviet prisoners, thousands of cattle and numerous heavy and individual weapons. In particular, numerous PPSh 41 submachine guns (Pistolet-Pulemët Špagina 1941) were captured, called by the Italians parabellum, who increased the firepower of the Black Shirts, almost without until then submachine guns.

The behavior of the Black Shirts was praised both by General Ewald von Kleist, commander of the I. Panzerarmee and by General Messe, commander of the C.S.I.R ..

The Petrikowka maneuver was one of the greatest successes achieved until then by the Italians since June 1940; in the Italian commands it gave considerable satisfaction to have succeeded alone where the Germans had failed, albeit with far greater means. Black Shirts and fanti had exceeded on this occasion the results obtained by the Panzergrenadiere of the Waffen SS. The Italian action was also praised in a letter sent by Adolf Hitler to the Duce on October 28th, 1941:

"The subsequent impact of the Kleist armored group for the formation of the bridgehead of Dnjepropetrowsk also gave your Divisions, Duce, the opportunity to carry out for the first time its own and completely victorious operation in the context of a great battle of annihilation".

The preconditions for pointing towards the Donetz mining and industrial basin, of great strategic importance, were fulfilled. Without allowing his departments to stop and rest, Kleist already on 8 October received and gave his troops the order to continue the advance in the dual director of Stalino and Taganrog on the Sea of Azov and then continue on Rostov. The Italian Expeditionary Force (CSIR) was to move to conquer Stalino together with the XLIX. Gebirgskorps: it was a matter of making a fast leap forward of over two hundred kilometers, for a front of a hundred, starting from a 150 km line deployment but with staggered Divisions at different depths, and equipped in an inorganic way.

The advance on Stalino began on the thirteenth. The *Tagliamento* the 16 was in Dimitrewka, managing to overcome the bridges interrupted by the Soviet spoilers and fighting both against the enemy rearguards, who exploited every hold available to slow the advance of the Axis, and against the rasputitza, the mud that transformed the steppe Ukrainian in an immense quagmire. In the late afternoon the Italians conquered the railway junction and the Stalino station, while the infantrymen of the 97. Infanteriedivision and the Gebirgsjäger of the 1.

Gebirgsdivision occupied the rest of the city. If Stalino was the nerve center of the Donetz region, Rykowo and Gorlowka also abounded in metallurgical and chemical installations that exploited the rich coal and metallurgical deposits that the area abounds with; and also, in nearby Trudowaja the Caspian oil pipeline opened. Taking it was therefore a strategic priority. Kleist ordered that the C.S.I.R. occupied the region; this time, however, the Italians would have operated without the support of the XLIX. Gebirgskorps who was to go to Rostov. On 28th October the legionaries of the of the 63rd *Tagliamento* Legion they reached Slawianka; on 29th Sergejewka; on November 1st they were in Grishino, and the advance continued. On November 5th, the *Tagliamento* reached Galijuzinowka and 11th Jussowa. On the same day the Legion left the dependencies of the *Pasubio* Division to switch to those of the 3rd *Celere*.

▲ Consul General Niccolò Nicchiarelli, commander of the Legion, then Group, Tagliamento.

▲ The Tagliamento Legion in Russia.

▼ Russian artillery post abandoned in a kolkhoz in the summer of 1941.

▲ Mussolini with Messe on the Russian front.

▲ Badge of the Legion Tagliamento 1941.

▼ Mussolini, Hitler and Messe review the CSIR, August 28th, 1941.

▲ Departure of the Leonessa Group.

▼ Mussolini, Hitler with Rundstet and Messe.

▲ Soviet anti-aircraft piece captured.

▲ Soviet prisoners captured in Petrikowka and sent to concentration camps.

▼ The advance continues. Black Shirts observe a column of CV35 wagons from the San Giusto Group.

▲ A CV33 wagon of the San Giorgio Group.

▲ A bridge destroyed by the retreating Soviets on the Dnieper.

▲ Black shirts of the Tagliamento legion with Russian civilians examine weapons captured from the Soviets in the summer of 1941.

▼ Soviet prisoners greet an Italian officer with a perfect fascist salute.

▲ Black Shirts in a front line village on the Dniepr.

▼ CCNN on the front line.

▲ A black shirt guarding an isba.

▲ Soviet T26 tank destroyed, summer 1941.

▼ Helmets and ammunition abandoned in the mud in Russia in the summer of 1941.

THE CHRISTMAS BATTLE (DECEMBER 1941)

After the capture of Gorlowka the only city of any importance still in Soviet hands was Nikitowka.

Colonel Chiaramonti, commander of the 80th *Roma* Infantry Regiment of *Pasubio* Division, having ascertained the presence of three Soviet Divisions in the area, took the initiative to occupy Nikitowka in order to reduce the gap between the C.S.I.R. and the German 17. Armee (von Stülpnagel), which was about fifty kilometers north.

Despite growing Soviet opposition, and despite losing contact with Italian troops, Chiaramonti continued to advance on Nikitowka, which he occupied, but in turn finding himself isolated and besieged by the 74th Riflemen Division, formed by the 189th and 360th Infantry Regiment and by the 307th Artillery.

A violent confrontation soon developed in the central part of the city. The infantrymen of the 80th managed to repel all the Soviet assaults, but the ammunition was running out to the point that it would have been impossible to attempt to re-enter the Italian lines.

He then decided to keep the positions pending help, thus preventing the Soviet infiltration of the leak between the C.S.I.R. and the 17. Armee.

Chiaramonti and his men endured six days, losing five hundred men; Messe described the resistance of the 80th infantry simply astonishing.

▲ The CCNN of the "Tagliamento" distribute food to Russian civilians.

▲ Wagons destroyed by Italians.

▼ Soviet flag captured.

To unlock Nikitowka and allow the 80th to return to the Italian lines between Gorlowka and Rikowo, it was decided to attempt an action with the 79th *Roma*, twin of the 80th, and elements of the *Lancieri di Novara* Regiment, supported by some pieces of the '8th Artillery Regiment. However, the Soviet reaction stopped the Italians and a counterattack forced them to abandon the action.

Two other attempts made on 10 and 11 November with two battalions of the 3rd *Bersaglieri* in support had no better results.

A new attempt took place on the 12th.

The spearhead of the operation was to be the 1st Company of the LXXIX° Black Shirt Assault Battalion of the *Tagliamento* that would have paved the way for the 79th Infantry.

On the morning of November 12th, also supported by the Italian fighters that used the Stalino airfield, the legionaries attacked the Soviet lines.

The assaults of the Black Shirts finally succeeded in opening a gap in the barrage of the besiegers, even if the Soviet pressure of the 74th Division did not diminish.

Elements of the 79th infantry then reached Nikitowka at 2.30 pm joining the 80th Regiment.

The Italians resisted until night, so under a blizzard the Chiaramonti troops and the forces that had helped him returned to the Italian lines.

The release of Nikitowka had cost the Italians one hundred and fifty dead, thirty-six missing and more than five hundred and fifty wounded; however with his truly heroic defense Chiaramonti had managed to prevent the enemy from infiltrating the Germans and the C.S.I.R . On December 7th the command of the *Tagliamento* was deployed to Krestowka.

▲ Black Shirts of the Tagliamento: Christmas battle.

The commander of the Legion was given command of the left side of the *Celere*. The nine Soviet troops attempted two coups against the positions held by the two battalions CC.NN.; another attempt was made on 13th December against the stronghold of Nowaja Orlowka, manned by the Friulian legionaries of the 2nd company of the LXXIX ° battalion who repelled the opposing patrols inflicting losses.

The increased action of Soviet patrols suggested that the Soviets were also planning an offensive in the sector held by the Italians.

Air reconnaissance and Italian patrols revealed the arrival of two Soviet Divisions (the 136th and 296th riflemen) in front of the *Celere*, as well as intense rail and vehicle traffic.

The Soviets were demonstrating a totally unexpected offensive recovery for the Wehrmacht's Oberkommando in those days. As early as November 29th, far from giving up, they had reoccupied Rostow; on December 10th the Red Army went on the attack on the north front, near Leningrad, forcing the Germans to retreat fifty kilometers. The offensive had extended to the central sector, where the Germans had to retreat a hundred kilometers without however the Soviets being able to reach Smolensk, the target set. In the southern sector, STAVKA set out to unhinge von Rundstedt's armies near Karkhov and then wrap the opposing armies deployed to the Black Sea and engaged in the Mius sector by a major attack that would have fixed them on the spot.

Finally, the cycle of operations should have culminated with the re-occupation of Chersonnese (Kersh), in Crimea, where Sevastopol continued to resist the Romanian-Germanic siege. The offensive, which began on January eighteen, failed these goals, only managing to create a large pocket in the sector of Isjum.

In this context, the Soviets had become very active after the sostitution of Budjenni with the general (later Marshal of the USSR) Timoshenko, and attacks were being launched against the sectors of the Mackensen Group (III. Ak), the XVe Ak, the XLIX Gebirgskorps and the CSIR, in search of the easiest direction of penetration, where to break through and operate in depth in order to force the Axis to commit its scarce reserves.

The Soviet reconnaissance with which the Black Shirts had clashed had served the Soviets to realize how scarce the troops were: five battalions of the 3rd *Bersaglieri* Regiment, four artillery groups and two battalions of the *Tagliamento*.

The political will to inflict a blow on Mussolini's fascist troops, the volunteers in black shirts, also had significant propaganda importance for the Soviets.

The politruk had given the order not to take the fascists prisoners, and other Italians also paid for the order, as when the Soviets massacred all the wounded of the 3rd *Bersaglieri* field hospital who fell into their hands.

It was also decided to attack on Christmas day, believing that the Italians that day were more depressed and afflicted by homesickness, moreover in the middle of the Russian winter, and therefore less inclined to fight. Probably a large part of the responsibility for this psychological lack of responsibility lies with the Italian communist refugees in Moscow, primarily Togliatti and D'Onofrio, who are particularly active in the defeatist propaganda directed to our soldiers at the front. At six o'clock in the morning on December 25th, a patrol of the 2nd company of the LXXIX ° commanded by the chief of staff Codeluppi left the stronghold of Nowaja Orlowka directed to Ploskj.

▲ Black Shirts during the Christmas battle.

▼ Black Shirts in action during the Christmas battle.

▲ Filippo Tommaso Marinetti in Russia.

A violent snow storm raged over the area, which lasted all day and prevented the Italian and Soviet aviation from taking part in the operations.

Leaving the stronghold Codeluppi noticed strong opposing groups, dressed in camou-flage suits, who, protected by the storm, were headed for Nowaja Orlowka and hurried back to the alarm.

These were the entire 1st and 2nd battalions of the 692th riflemen Regiment of the 296th Infantry Division, who began the attack both frontally and on the left side of the stronghold, supported by two artillery Regiments (530th and 813th), and various mortar units.

The attack was very hard, and at 7.30 the centurion Mengoli sent his last radio message to the Legion command:

We are attached to the front and to the left. Reinforcements are needed.

After this message the connections with Nowaja Orlowka broke off.

The attacking battalions also joined the cavalrymen of the 38th cavalry Division, supported by artillery and fire from 102mm mortars. The company commander, centurion Mengoli, had fallen, all the officers were dead or injured when the chief officer Ezio Barale, the only officer left, at the climax of the clash, ordered a counterattack on the white weapon with a handful of survivors. Separated from his own, he fought with his dagger until he was killed by a shot.

At 6.30 the 3rd battalion of the 692nd Soviet Regiment, belonging to the 296th riflemen Division, preceded by cavalry units and supported by artillery (a Regiment) and 102mm mortars, attacked the stronghold of Malo Orlowka, held by the Friulians of the LXIII th battalion Black Shirts, but the reaction of the soldiers was very hard, and the Soviet attack was nipped with heavy losses.

▲ *'Rukij Verk! Hands up!'* Ransacking of 'M' legionnaires in a Soviet village.

A column of the 136th, circumvented Ivanovka, headed towards Mikhailowka, held by the Black Shirts of the LXXIX ° battalion. The clash became fierce, so much so that the Black Shirts also defended themselves with daggers - Marshal Messe wrote that the fight is very hard, with frequent clashes with the baionets - and the commander of the *Tagliamento*, Consul Nicchiarelli, ordered the dispatch in reinforcement of the 2nd company of the LXIII ° battalion (centurion De Apollonia) which was located in Malo Orlowka, ten kilometers away. De Apollonia and his men, however, were attacked by a battalion of the 692th riflemen with at least six hundred men, and had to fall back on Krestowka.

Meanwhile, the Soviets began to massacre the wounded of the 18th-century field hospital where Bersaglieri and legionaries returning from Nowaja Orlowka were hospitalized; the first to be killed was the second lieutenant Angelo Vidoletti who tried to defend the wounded (he had the Golden Medal in memory), then the others were massacred one by one with a blow to the back of the neck.

He was a wounded, successful Bersagliere managed to escape and hidden by a Ukrainian woman, to tell the story of the events when, forty-eight hours after Ivanovka, she was taken back by the Italians. In judging the treatment inflicted by the Germans on Soviet prisoners, episodes like this, far from uncommon, should be evaluated.

At 15.45 also Krestowka and the command of the *Tagliamento* were attacked by the 296th Division and by the cavalry of the 38th Division; apart from the command platoon the only force available for defense was the company of centurion De Apollonia who had taken refuge there after being attacked in the morning. Given the increasing pressure, the Legion commander decided to fall back on Malo Orlowka, who continued to resist.

Thus was formed a flying column formed by the command of the *Tagliamento*, by the platoon command of the LXIII ° battalion accompanying weapons, protected by the 2nd company of the LXIII ° battalion CC.NN.; the column was also joined by the II ° Group of the Horse Artillery Regiment with a section of 20 guns.

The column opened the way to Malo Orlowka, covered by the men of D'Apollonia and artillery on horseback in the rear.

The situation immediately became heavy, as the Soviets pressed on the 2nd company, supported by the zero-lift shot of one of the Voloire (Horse- Artillery) batteries, which together with the intense fire of the Black Shirts forced the enemy to fall back, so much so that the gunners, once exhausted the ammunition, they could attach the pieces to the pairs by resuming the movement towards Malo Orlowka which was reached at 5.30 pm.

In the night, the command of the C.S.I.R. and that of the XLIX. Gebirgskorps decided to go on the counteroffensive the following day, reoccupying Ivanovka and Nowo Orlowka.

In addition to the Italians, the XLIX mobile reserve would also be used, consisting of Infanterieregiment 318., a few wagons of the Panzerregiment 10. (mostly Pzkw IIIG and H, in addition to a few Pzkw IVE) and Fallschirmjägerregiment 2. (whose use however had not yet been authorized).

What mattered most, as Marshal Messe later wrote, was that:

"At the end of the first day of battle, the enemy attack was clearly curbed and our reaction to restore the situation has already started satisfactorily"

▲ Portrait of Filippo Tommaso Marinetti wearing the MVSN uniform in Russia.

▲ Legionnaires of the Group "Tagliamento" and Croatian Black Shirts, Russian front 1942.

▼ Commander Egon Zitnik with other officers of the Croatian Legion of MVSN. Note the initial use of Yugoslavian uniform with Italian exhibitions.

▲ The commander of the Croatian Legion of MVSN Egon Zitnic (center). Right: Badge of the Croatian Legion of MVSN, with the Italian and Croatian coats of arms, the Beam and the Ustasha symbol, and the sketches *FOR THE DUCE ALALA' and ZA DOM SPREMNI!* (For the Fatherland, come on!)

▼ Black Shirt Gunners in the Steppe

On the morning of December 26th the Italian-German counterattack resumed; however the Soviets had not given up hope of breaking through, and the attacks in the *Tagliamento* sector reiterated.

Supported by almost all the panzers of the Panzerregiment 10. the *Bersaglieri* of the XVIII battalion and two battalions (1. and 22.) of the Infanterieregiment 318. re-employed Orlowko Ivanovka, excluding the northern side of the village.

In the meantime, the panzers arrived at the hill 331.7 and managed to snatch it from the 964th Riflemen Regiment, holding it for a while, but eventually being rejected by the growing opposing pressure.

As for the *Tagliamento*, the LXIII ° battalion CC.NN. he came out of the Malo Orlowka stronghold to try to regain the positions of Nowaja Orlowka lost in the previous day.

As the Black Shirts advanced under the storm, they were suddenly attacked by troops of the 962nd infantry and cavalry (Cossacks of the 68th Cavalry div.) from Krestowka, who were moving to attack Malo Orlowka.

The LXIII ° quickly retreated to the starting positions, from where he managed to push the Soviets back, inflicting heavy losses at 962nd.

Also the LXXIX ° battalion CC.NN. and the XVIII *Bersaglieri* remained in defense of the Mikhailowka stronghold were hit by at least two Soviet battalions (II° / 733 , III / 966th and perhaps also troops of the 387th Riflemen) supported by the shooting of mortars from 102nd and artillery.

The Black Shirts resisted the assaults, until the arrival of some Pzkw III E of the Panzerregiment 10. returning from Ivanovka forced the Soviet riflemen to disengage.

In the afternoon, however, the Soviets unleashed a violent counterattack, rejecting the Germans first and then the Italians out of the town.

On the twenty-sixth day it closed without particular success on the Italian-German side.

On the morning of the twenty-seventh the weather had definitely improved.

This allowed both the Soviet Air Force and the 22nd autonomous fighter group to make their appearance on the skies of the battlefield.

The Macchi C.200 fighters had a good game against the I-16b, decidedly older aircraft and that the Italian pilots, in many cases veterans of the Spanish conflict, knew well. In three days the 22nd could claim fourteen wins.

That day it was decided that the *Tagliamento* Legion would repeat the failed attack the previous day; to strengthen the Black Shirts they were assigned to the LIII Battalion CC.NN. by Primo Seniore Ermacora Zuliani the mortars of the A.A. of the 81st Torino Infantry Regiment.

A battalion of the same Regiment would have flanked flanked protecting the left side of the CC.NN battalion.

The action began in the early morning, and the soldiers, assisted by the infantrymen and elements of the other battalion of the Legion, the LXXIX ° CC.NN., who moved from Mikhailowka, re-occupied the positions of Nowaja Orlowka towards noon.

At fifteen, after an intense machine-gunning and breaking up carried out by the 22nd Group, the Black Shirts together with the German infantrymen of 318. They were able to recapture Ivanovka, where they discovered the massacre of the prisoners and the wounded carried out by the riflemen of the 296th on the 25th.

The offensive thrust of Timoshenko's troops was now exhausted. This did not mean, however, that the Soviets had given up fighting.

In fact, during the night two battalions of the 964th of the 296th riflemen supported by elements of the 733rd / 136th attacked snatching 331.7 altitude forcing the Germans to fall back within the Z Line.

On the morning of 28 the Consul Nicchiarelli, commander of the *Tagliamento*, assumed command of the reserve of the 3rd Division *Celere* Amedeo duke of Aosta.

The situation created by the loss of the 331.7 share meant that the command of the XLIX Gebirgskorps, on which *Celere* was operationally dependent, ordered its recon-quest. At half past nine in the morning the LXIII ° Black Shirts battalion moved to conquer the altitude, held by the 964th Regiment of the 296th and by elements of the 733rd belonging to the 136th Riflemen Division.

The legionnaires of Zuliani were supported by two Panzerkampfwagen III H of Panzerregiment 10, by two platoons of 81 mortars and by two platoons of 47/32 cannons of the LXIII ° battalion A.A. Sassari della *Tagliamento*, and the 81st mortar platoon.

After the preliminary bombing done by the mortar companies, the Black Shirts attacked first with a dense throw of hand grenades and then with the white weapon, and despite the numerical inferiority at noon the hill 311, 7 was firmly in Italian hand, while the Russian riflemen quickly retreated to Woroshilowa.

Taking advantage of the favorable moment, Zuliani ordered the continuation of the action pressing on the enemy and at sixteen the village of Woroshilowa was conquered by the Black Shirts of Udine.

At that point the Soviets launched the 733rd and 964th against Woroshilowa, without however being able to dislodge the soldiers, in whose hands the village remained firmly.

On December 29 the Soviets continued to attack to retake Woroshilowa to the Black Shirts of the LXIII °; the fight was fierce but the Friulian legionaries held until the arrival of the comrades of the LXXIX ° CC.NN. coming from Ivanovka.

Even on the morning of 30, before dawn, the 296th made another attempt to resume Woroshilowa, but the *Tagliamento* promptly repelled all attacks; however, the Soviet infantrymen seized the 331.7 share, held by two platoons of the InfRgt 318, which left the *Tagliamento* isolated in Woroshilowa.

Given the temperature, which went down to -35, even the radios could not work.

Consul Nicchiarelli decided to attempt the opening of a passage with two daring pla-toons, but the violent concentration of fire prevented the platoons from leaving the country.

At seven in the morning, a daring platoon came out commanded by Menegozzo, who reached 331.7, seizing it with a coup that took the Soviets totally by surprise.

Menegozzo then managed to reach the village of Ivanovskiy, connecting with the deputy commander of *Celere* and exposing the situation in which the Black Shirts were.

An action was then decided which preceded the unblocking of Woroshilowa and the reconquest of quota 331.7.

This action would have been carried out by the Division's reserve battalion, the XVIII *Bersaglieri* battalion, supported by the few Pz III H tanks of the PzRgt 10.

However, when *Bersaglieri* and tankers reached 331.7, they were surprised to find it not in

Soviet hands but guarded by the *Tagliamento*'s Black Shirts that had occupied it after the coup of the platoon of Menegozzo, thus alleviating the situation in Woroshilowa.

The Christmas battle was over. Timoshenko's offensive had been nipped from the start thanks to the determination of the Black Shirts of the *Tagliamento* Legion and the *Bersaglieri* of the XVIII ° who had not succumbed in very difficult climatic situations (- 43 °, under storms of snow) against a much more numerous enemy.

▲ An MVSN car column crosses an urban centre.

▲ The Black Shirts conquer Stalino.

▼ M Legionaries in action at Stalino, summer 1942.

▲ Transit of Italian motor vehicles in a population centre in Russia.

▼ Black Shirts storming a village.

▲ Ukraine: Black Shirts in combat on a river floodplain.

▲ Ukraine: Black Shirts in combat.

▲ The prisoners are coming out of the isbas.

▼ The Soviet prisoners.

▲ Two Soviet soldiers surrender.

▲ Black shirts forward.

▲ Lunch is eaten on a decapitated statue of Lenin.

▼ Lunch on the statue of Lenin.

THE RAGGRUPPAMENTO 3 GENNAIO AND THE FIRST DEFENSIVE BATTLE OF DON RIVER (AUGUST 1943)

In the meantime, the *Raggruppamento* (Battlegroup) d'Assalto CC.NN. *3 Gennaio* under the command of Lieutenant General Filippo Diamanti (the same whose Black Shirts had fought strenuously in the defense of Passo Uarieu during the 1st battle of Tembien during the Italo-Ethiopian War, in January 1936, saving with their resistance the whole Italian deployment from encirclement).

It was the first of the two *Raggruppamenti* which were expected to be used in the USSR, together with the *Raggruppamento 23 Marzo*; for the time being, the *3 Gennaio* Group was made up only of the departments of the *Tagliamento* Group and the Croatian Black Shirts of the Croatian Legion, while the other component, the *Montebello* Group, would only come online on 11 September; the *Raggruppamento* Command came instead in August. The *Raggruppamento* (that is, in practice the *Tagliamento* Group and the thousand Croatian legionaries) operated within the XXXV Corps, of which it was a troop available to the Command, together with the Mounted Battlegroup *Barbò*, *Raggruppamento a cavallo Barbò*, and the veteran Divisions of the old C.S.I.R. *Celere*, Pasubio and *Torino*, to which was added the newly arrived *Sforzesca* who had not yet had the baptism of fire in Russia, and a series of minor departments including the 32nd *Compagnia Controcarro Granatieri di Sardegna*, particularly chosen.

The troops of Messe had to preside over a sector over sixty kilometers long as the crow flies, but in reality along the banks full of loops of the Don the deployment had to cover eighty; this sector was delimited to the west by the Jelanskoie meridian and to the east by the point corresponding to where, on the opposite shore, the Choper river flows into the Don.

The *Sforzesca* Division constituted with its 54th *Umbria* infantry the right wing of the whole deployment (and putting non-practical troops of the Russian front in such an important position was a mistake paid then painfully). To the right of the *Sforzesca* was the 79. Infanteriedivision, belonging to the 17. *Armeekorps* of the gen. Hollidt, far left wing of the 6. Armee of General d. Panzertruppe Frederich Paulus. For an extension of about thirty kilometers to the east on the right bank of the Don, from the point overlooking the point where the Choper flows into the Don up to the wide loop that the Don forms in Serafimovitch, the surveillance of the shore was entrusted only to an exploration group formed by a cavalry squadron (Conforti column), a cyclist company and a pioneer company, distributed in a few kilometers of backward barriers very far from the river and widely spaced between them. In fact, the command of the Army Group B had considered that the Don was untreatable in that stretch and considered the area safe. In such a situation, the Soviets ended up finding themselves masters not only of the left bank of the river, but also of the right, where they continued to hold the bridgehead of Serafimovitch's loop and that of the forest between Bobrowskj and Baskowskj, from where they launched continuous attacks of patrols against the Italians, but also of the villages of the coastal strip, from which they had gone extending deeply towards the south especially near the junction line between the *Sforzesca* and the German 79. Inf.Div.. Given the very uncertain tactical contact situation between the Italian XXXV Corps and the German AK 17., the Soviet troops had an excellent starting point for conducting attacks and offensive bets against the XXXV Corps.

To parry the threat, Messe ordered that the Corps reserves commanded by Gen. C. Pellegrini included the 53rd and 54th *Umbria* Infantry Regiment and the 17th Motorized Artillery Regiment. On August 6th Hollidt, commander of the 17th AK (on which *Celere* temporarily depended) ordered two *Bersaglieri* battalions (XIII ° and XIX ° both of the 6th) and two Germans (1./208. and 3./212, 79. InfDiv.) To rake the forest by the Russians of the 304th Division, despite the unfavorable opinion of the *Celere* command. Despite hours of individual fighting in the forests, and despite having reached the banks of the Don at two points, the Italian-Germans had to retreat after Soviet assault troops had managed to infiltrate the Axis positions at night. of the Army, that is the Black Shirts of the 3 *Gennaio* (excluding the Croatian Legion, which passed to the tactical dependencies of the Pasubio Division) and the Mounted Battlegroup *Barbò* gravitated to the right of the deployment. The command of the *Sforzesca* Division also provided to protect its line by deploying two battalions of the 54th infantry facing north towards the bank of the Don, and arranging the third front to the east to face a possible infiltration on the side. On August 15th, the *Tagliamento* Group was located as follows:

Bolschoj: Command Grouping 3 *Gennaio*;
Bolschoj: *Tagliamento* Group Command;
Bolschoj: LXXX ° btg. M (except one company);
Blinoff: LXIII ° btg. M;
Kowoskij: a company of the LXXIX ° btg. M.

Diamanti tried to connect with the 79. Infanteriedivision and was disappointed to discover that the occupation of the sector did not lend itself to defense as regards observation, being made up of small isolated nuclei, and also that the villages of Brobrowskij and Ust Choperskij on the banks of the Don, near the junction between the 17. German and the *Sforzesca* were in the hands of the Soviets. Between 12th and 20th August the enemy carried out, as always before an offensive, some raids against the Italian side, which, although limited in scope, cost the Italians a dozen deaths and numerous injuries.

The aim was to identify the weakest point of the deployment to attempt a breakthrough: this point was identified in the sector held by the 54th Regiment of the *Sforzesca*. On the morning of August 17th, the command of the XXXV Corps warned the 3 *Gennaio* Cluster of the increasing Soviet activity from the Serafimovitch loop to the west and south. The transfer of the Command of the *Tagliamento* Group and of the LXIII ° battalion M from Bolschoj and Blinoff to Dewjatkin was then ordered and the grouping of the LXXIX ° M with its own company advanced in Kotowskij; the command of the Battlegroup also moved to Dewjatkin, and took over the 1st battery of the 201st Motorized Artillery Regiment

At 2.30 in the morning of August 20, the Soviets attacked the 54th *Umbria* Regiment with three Regiments of the 197th riflemen Division, the 828th, 862nd and 889th infantry. These were troops ferried on the bank of the Don in the sector that the Italians believed presided over by the *Landser* of the Inf. Regt. 79., but which they had left unattended without warning the command of *Sforzesca*. Fighting took place in particular in the infantrymen village of Simowsky, who managed to repel two Soviet attacks.

▲ Messe with the Black Shirts of the 'Tagliamento', 1941.

▼ Messe with the legionnaires of the Tagliamento Group.

▲ Soviet T26 wagon captured by Italians.

A third attack began at seven, penetrating the lines of the second battalion and putting him to flight, and bypassing and attacking the villages of Simowskij and Krutowskij behind him, and at eight thirty the 1st battalion of the 54th evacuated the sector of Simowskij. Of 684 men, only 72 returned to the Italian lines. The situation forced the III ° / 54 °, already deployed facing east, to be engaged online, which was taken over by the LXIII ° battalion M that Messe had made available to the command of the *Sforzesca*.

The LXIII ° M immediately took a position facing north east along the edge of the balka which from Krutowskij heads south; the action of the Black Shirts was joined by the dragoons of 3rd *Savoia Cavalleria* from the Conforti column and a horse-drawn battery; what managed to prevent the riflemen of the 19th from spreading behind the *Sforzesca* by circumscribing the enemy occupation pending a counterattack to eliminate it. To this end, Messe also placed the LXXIX ° battalion M and the 1st battery of the 201 ° Artillery under the control of the *Sforzesca* Division. It was not until 3:30 pm, thirteen hours after the attack, that the 2nd battalion of the 54th managed to escape the encirclement. The veterans remembered how everywhere they saw fugitives of the 54th Regiment: for this reason the Soviets disdainfully renamed the *Sforzesca* Cikay divizijon, flight-Division.

l Galbiati, Chief of Staff of M.V.S.N. and Francisci, Group Commander 23 March.

Meanwhile the Soviets continued to ferry men from the left bank, including elite troops from the 14th Division of the Guards.

At eighteen in the afternoon the Black Shirts of the LXXIX ° M arrived at the location indicated on the Italian maps as Le Fontanelle (the springs), two kilometers south of the altitude 163.1, while the 1st battery of the 201 ° took up a position nearby by placing the pieces in the battery .

At dawn the following day the Soviets resumed attacking between 54th and 53rd infantry at the welding spot, with fresh departments of the 14th Guards and 204th riflemen, pointing in the direction of altitude 232.2, the central node of the displuvial between Kriutscha and Zuzkan.

At 11.50 in the morning, the LXXIX ° Battalion M received the order to move with the trucks to 232, 2 altitude and from here move on foot to occupy the 191, 4 and 188.6 quotas still believed to be clear, settling in defense. Arriving around 15.00 near the point established to get off the trucks, the column head vehicles were hit by the 232.2m fire which had been occupied by the Soviets. The battalion command decided to attack, but at the same time the riflemen of the 889th Regiment tried to circumvent the battalion, which managed to cope with the situation, but around 17.30 later in intense mortar fire, regardless of the losses suffered, the riflemen returned to launch a violent attack to try to repeat the circumvention on the right side of the Black Shirts.

▲ Galbiati and Francisci speak at the 23 Marzo Grouping leaving for the front.

▲ The M legionnaires of the Montebello Group leaving for the eastern front, 1942.

▼ Francisci and Galbiati.

The situation became critical for the enemy pressure and for the loss of several men including several officers (only four remained); the ammunition was also running low, and the battalion command was aware of the excessive dispersion of forces on a too large front: but a retreat to better defensible positions would have left the two highly proven battalions of the 54th and the artillery in the mercy of the enemy folding. The commander of the LXXIX ° M ordered to continue the resistance on the site, without giving in a meter, and the Black Shirts continued to protect the retreat of the *Sforzesca* troops, with an angry and heroic resistance. The action of the LXXIX ° had drawn all the attention of the Russians to the ward, who tended to break the Italian lineup in order to then circumvent the sections.

While the LXXIX ° battalion was engaged in the fighting, Messe had meanwhile ordered the command of the *Sforzesca* to constitute a cornerstone at the town of Tchebotarewskij by bringing all the troops available in the right sector of the Division, including the LXIII ° battalion. CC.NN. M with the LXIII ° battalion A..A., the Colonna Conforti (*Savoia Cavalleria* and horse-drawn artillery) in addition to the survivors of the 1st battalion of the 54th Regiment. The command of the LXIII ° M and the remains of the I° / 54° was given to Lieutenant Colonel Vittorio De Franco, commander of the LXIII ° Battalion of Sassari accompanying weapons of the *Tagliamento* Group. Around 18.30 the Soviets became aware of the movement, and sent elements of the 19th and 14th Guards against the right flank of the 1st Battalion of the 54th Infantry, who wedged themselves between this and the LXIII Battalion M, which was deployed along a defensive perimeter of five kilometers.

The 1st Battalion was wiped out, while the Black Shirts of the LXIII, also isolated, managed to break through taking advantage of the growing darkness and reach Tchebotarewskij. The Colonna Conforti had been cut off from the break-up of the Soviets in the gap between infantrymen and Black Shirts, but the Dragoons swarmed the riflemen, putting them on the run and opening a gap together with the Horse- artillery, but suffering serious losses.

The legionaries of the LXXIX° M witnessed the clashes, without however being able to intervene both because they were heavily engaged and for the mixing of the Italian and Soviet troops. If the Soviets had managed to disorganize the retreat of the Italians, they failed to obtain tactical results, because at night the Italian departments succeeded, under the protection offered by the LXXIX° M that continued to fight, to reorganize themselves and take a position in Tchebotarewskij.

These few lines in their schematic do not do justice to the behavior of the legionaries, behavior that earned the Labaro of the Group the Golden Medal for Military Valor, therefore forgive us a rather long quote that well describes what happened. In a re-enactment of the battle, a veteran of the glorious *Savoia Cavalleria* gives a vivid description of the battles sustained by the Black Shirts of the LXXIX° M Battalion on the night of August 21st, statement that is worth reporting in full:

Meanwhile those of the Tagliamento continued to resist under the blows: decimated, destroyed, in pieces, but miraculously they still held on. We heard distinctly says Gualtiero Lolli, (...) commandant of the II Squadroon [of Savoia Cavalleria, Author's Note] (...) in the roar of the fight the shouts - of the Urra Stalin shouts - of the Russians who were going to attack. It was already night, but because of the mortars and machine guns it was seen as day: they were massacring them all....

Those of the Tagliamento, therefore, pay personally the collapse of the Sforzesca.

They are four cats, who with fingernails and teeth defend themselves angrily.

In the darkness torn by lightning, a helmet is occasionally glimpsed above the fray, against which the enemy tracers rage.

Armed with a musket, the unknown one still finds the strength to carefully aim, looking at the direction from which the tracers arrive; shoots and hits, shoots and hits, without interruption, until he also falls on the corpse of the others, of the comrades ".

"How much longer, for a miraculous willpower, the struggle of the guys of the Tagliamento, with much greater anger, the Russians are raging over those positions [to the riflemen of the 889th Regiment, 197th Division, rates had also been added in the meantime of the 14th Riflemen Division of the Guards, Authors's Note].

You can clearly see them rushing in droves, in that dark [broken] by the blinding flashes, by the flashes that turn the sky bluish and yellow, with the smoke of the bursts to reflect bizarrely the flash of explosions. The Russians seem drunk, so much they get underneath, they throw themselves running with the parabellum shaken from right to left to vomit tracers. The fans of the trajectories make curious light effects, geometric embroidery, barely parabolic lines, when the blow is lost far away.

Like cats from seven lives, the brave ones resist Russian.

In spasmodic haste there is no time to distinguish between those who come forward by shooting and those who raise their hands in surrender: it can be a trick to make you stick your nose out of the hole and lie down dry. So you shoot as long as you can, as long as there are ammunition or you are killed as beasts by the advancing enemy".

In fact, vodka was often given before Soviet assaults.

▲ The Group 23 Marzo deployed in Saluzzo before departure for the eastern front.

"The flashes of cannon shots rose from the balkes, "says Nino Malingambi, also of the II Squadron,."We heard distinctly shouting: Mommy! Help! Savoy! Italy! ... They were those of the Tagliamento who had received the order not to fall back anyway. (...)"

The resistance of the soldiers of the LXXIX° had prevented the Soviet riflemen of the 889th Regiment and the 14th Guards from wrapping the right wing of the Italian deployment. The legionaries had lived up to their hymn until the end, really fighting, as their hymn said, until the last breath.

As General Messe acknowledged, commander of the XXXV Army Corps (the old CSIR) speaking of the Black Shirts of the LXXIX °, it was due to the conscious sacrifice of his soldiers if the enemy, as a result of the arrest he suffered, was unable to overcome the right wing of the deployment that in the late afternoon.

The fighting lasted until late at night, when the hundred surviving legionnaires of the LXXIX managed to reach Tchebotarewskij fighting at 2.30 on the night of August 22nd, attending to defend this stronghold together with the troops already present at five in the morning. The day of August 22nd passed without the Soviets attacking the positions of the *Tagliamento* Group and other departments entrenched in Tchebotarewskij.

It was only towards the early hours of the night that departments of the 203rd Division silently approached the sector held by the Black Shirts of the LXXIX Battalion, who, having noticed the opposing patrols, promptly invested them with the shooting of their weapons and then started to counterattack at the white weapon, to avoid running out of increasingly scarce ammunition, rejecting the Soviets, who during the night then tried several times to infiltrate without achieving any result and always being thrown back by the soldiers.

At 3.30 on 23rd August the 203rd riflemen attacked in force across the board, being contained by the Italians at the cost of huge losses.

Italians and a worrying consumption of ammunition, in the process of exhaustion. Just the ammunition was what worried the legionaries: men, for three days have not rested, for two days have not eaten, but only ask for ammunition.

At ten o'clock in the morning the 612th Regiment of the 203rd Division launched a new violent attack, rejected by the Black Shirts, which they had the joy of seeing arrive shortly after the expected ammunition. The Soviets attacked again in force (now with departments of the 14th Guards) on the afternoon of the 23rd, being rejected once again. In the afternoon patrols of explorers from the *Tagliamento* came out and returned after taking some prisoners, from which the names of the departments used by the enemy and the huge number of deaths caused by the resistance of the legionaries were learned. The same evening, since the *Tagliamento* Group was now fully assembled in Tchebotarewskij, the command of the *Sforzesca* Division, with the consent of Messe, authorized the Consul Mittica to resume direct command of his Group, whose departments had hitherto been used separately as a reserve under the XXXV Corps and the Division command. If in other sectors the day of the 24th was very hard (the *Savoia Cavalleria* Regiment carried out the famous charge of Isbushenskij that day en route three battalions of the 802nd / 304th Riflemen) in Tchebotarewskij the day passed quietly, allowing the Black Shirts to rest even if in a state of continuous vigilance.

In reality, the Soviets were preparing the decisive attack on the stronghold, an attack that was

▲ Legionnaires M on a direct line to Russia, 1942.

triggered by the 203rd and 14th Guards Division at five thirty in the morning on August 25th.

The Soviets attacked Tchebotarewskij with forces estimated to be tenfold than those of the defenders, wrapping Italian positions from the east and cutting off the departments from any direct contact with the commands and with the artillery units intended to support the defenses.

The artillery also, following the winding, was found to be deprived of the protection of the infantry, so that they had to reposition themselves south of Kotowsky where Savoy Cavalry and Lancers of Novara were located. Despite the Soviet pressure, the *Tagliamento* Group's Black Shirts and the infantrymen of the 1st Battalion of the 54th *Umbria* resisted for hours; the legionaries, as in the previous days, to better target and save ammunition by shooting without fail they stood up to fire regardless of the bursts.

But the heavy losses, the depletion of ammunition, the total lack of water and the interrupted connections finally led to Mittica and the ten.col. Spighi to order a sortie to the south west, in an attempt to reach Gorbatowo, or if impossible, any area held by Axis troops.

Three columns were formed: on the left the Black Shirts of the LXXIX M, in the center the LXIII Battalion M and elements of the LXIII Battalion accompanying weapons, on the right the remains of the 1st Battalion of the 54th Infantry of the *Sforzesca*. The three columns attacked the besiegers with a furious throw of grenades and a white weapon, opening a passage through which they managed to pass all the survivors, even if injured, also carrying most of the bodies of the fallen so as not to leave them in hand to the enemy.

The Soviets chased the three columns, but the rear guards, in order to delay the pursuers, marked the white weapon, having exhausted all ammunition, having now fired to the last cartridge. Finally the columns of Black Shirts and foot soldiers, with Mittica and Spighi at the head, managed to disengage, reaching in the late afternoon to the village of Gorbatowo, where General Pellegrini was with the command of the *Sforzesca* Division.

Here finally supplied with ammunition, water and provisions, Black Shirts and infantrymen placed themselves at the disposal of the divisional command for the defense of Gorbatowo against the repeated enemy attacks, which ceased only the following day, on August 26th.

The overall losses of the Battaglioni CC.NN. M *Tagliamento* in the days from 20-26th August 1942 were of 458 men.

During the operating cycle, the Black Shirts had captured 3 82 mortars, 4 heavy machine guns, 8 PTRD 41 anti-tank rifles, 16 machine guns, 7 PPSh submachine guns, 150 Tokarev M 40 automatic rifles, ammunition and various material as well as 445 prisoners, including 4 official. On the morning of the twenty-sixth the *Tagliamento* Group was reduced to a total strength of 14 officers and 420 Black Shirts (in July, after the battle of Krasnij Lutsch it consisted of 60 officers and 1503 between non-commissioned officers and soldiers). The Group was lined up on the ridges northwest of Gorbatowo. The *Sforzesca* command ordered it to move north east in order to occupy and preside over the locality of altitude 228, on the ridge between the valleys of Kriuscha and Zuzkan; but when the *Tagliamento* reached the altitude it found it already manned by the Soviets.

It was then taken to occupy and garrison the stretch in front of it, fifteen kilometers long, which was occupied by groups connected to each other by mobile patrols armed with automatic weapons, mostly captured by the Soviets.

▲ The departing Black Shirts get on the train.

▼ Distribution of the war bulletin.

The situation remained unchanged the following day, until the morning of the twenty-eighth of August, when a platoon of the LXXIX M sent on reconnaissance managed to take hold of a hand of altitude 228, taking the Soviets by surprise.

The Black Shirts organized the first defense of the altitude until they were taken over by the infantrymen of the 1st Battalion of the 54th infantry. The riflemen of the 14th Guards attempted several times to regain the altitude, and on August 30th the Consul Mittica had to send Baradello to relieve the the infantrymen, at the head of a company of Black Shirts of the LXIII M; as soon as it arrived, the company launched a counterattack by capturing some prisoners and automatic weapons.

The opposing pressure, however, surrounded 228 share cutting it off the Italian lines. On August 31st, the 4th Tridentina Alpine Division arrived in the area, which caused the Soviet retreat.

On September 1st, the Soviets stopped all offensive operations.

On September 2nd, the *Tagliamento* Group, now bled to death, was withdrawn from the front line and transferred to the divisional reserve to be restored with the arrival of accessories and materials.

On 11th September, the other Battalion Group of the Group, *Montebello*, also quickly arrived from Krasnaja Saria, sent quickly from Italy due to the situation at the front. On September 28, the ceremony with which von Weichs, commander of the Army Group B, intended to reward the victorious resistance of the XXXV Corps was held in Gorbatowo; forty Class II Iron Crosses were conferred, two thirds of which went to the *Tagliamento* Group's Black Shirts; Messe received the Knight's Cross (Ritterkreuz). The General der Infanterie von Tippelskirch, representing von Weichs addressed words of praise and stoma to the departments deployed.

In the same ceremony Gariboldi decorated the Labaro of the *Tagliamento* Group with the

▲ Reading the war bulletin to the Black Shirts.

Golden Medal for Military Valor for the behavior of the legionaries of the LXXIX on the 232.2 level.

The *Tagliamento* and *Montebello* groups formed the CC.NN. Assault Battlegroup 3 *Gennaio*. Commanders: Lieutenant General Filippo Diamanti; then Consul General Alessandro Lusana. As part of the expansion of the Italian military presence on the eastern front, which led to the creation of the Italian Army in Russia, it was decided to increase the number of MVSN units present, both for the excellent evidence provided by the 63rd *Tagliamento* Legion in the fighting of the 1941, both for the political significance of the presence of openly fascist units in the struggle against the Soviet communist regime.

In this context, the establishment of a Grouping was formed consisting of the first M battalions formed in 1941, and which took the name of March 23rd, which took the name of the Militia Divisions that had fought in East Africa in 1935-36, in Spain and in Northern Africa in 1941. It is also very probable that this name was a tribute to the designated commander, Lieutenant General Enrico Francisci, one of the best officers of the MVSN, who in Spain had previously commanded the Banderas Grouping of the same name at Guadalajara, where he it was distinct, and then the Volunteer Division *23 Marzo*. As the *Raggruppamento 3 Gennaio* was intended to be assigned to the 25th Army Corps, so on *23 Marzo* it would in turn operate within the II Corps, also about to be sent to Russia, in order to strengthen the two large units with two real Divisions, albeit small but formed by assault troops. The *Raggruppamento 23 Marzo* was allegedly divided into two CC.NN. M Battalion groups, the Valle Scrivia Group and the Leonessa Group:

Gruppo Battaglioni CC.NN. M d'Assalto Leonessa
Comandante: Console Generale Graziano Sardu (KiA)
XIV° Btg. CC.NN. M (Bergamo): Seniore Comincioli (KiA)
XV° Btg. CC.NN. M (Brescia): Seniore Albonetti
XXXVIII° Btg. Armi d'Accompagnamento CC.NN. M (Asti): Seniore Vannini

Gruppo Battaglioni CC.NN. M d'Assalto Valle Scrivia
Comandante: Console Generale Mario Bertoni -
V° Btg. CC.NN. M (Tortona): Primo Seniore Masper (KiA)
XXXIV° Btg. CC.NN. M (Savona): Seniore Gloria (WiA)
XLI° Btg. Armi d'Accompagnamento CC.NN. M (Trento): ?

As told, the groups Leonessa and Valle Scrivia formed the Ragruppamento d'Assalto CC.NN. *23 Marzo*.

Commanders: Lieutenant General Enrico Francisci; Lieutenant General Edgardo Preti (interim); Lieutenant General Martinesi.

▲ A very young Legionnaire gets on the train...

▲... Followed by his head man

▲ Roman greetings... And more!

▼ Departure for the front. Battalion flame.

▲ The grouping mules on the wagon headed for the front.

▼ General Enrico Francisci with the Bolzano federal officer Vittorio Passalacqua.

▲ Francisci with the Federal Vittorio Passalacqua and members of the Fascist women's organisations at the Bolzano railway station.

▼ General Enrico Francisci, General Arturo Taranto, the Bolzano Federal Councillor Vittorio Passalacqua and the Prefect of Bozen/Bolzano passed the picket of honour at the Bolzano railway station.

▲ Bolzano railway station. Fruit distributed to soldiers leaving for Russia.

▼ Bolzano railway station. Distribution of fruit by the women's organizations of the PNF to the 'M' legionnaires leaving.

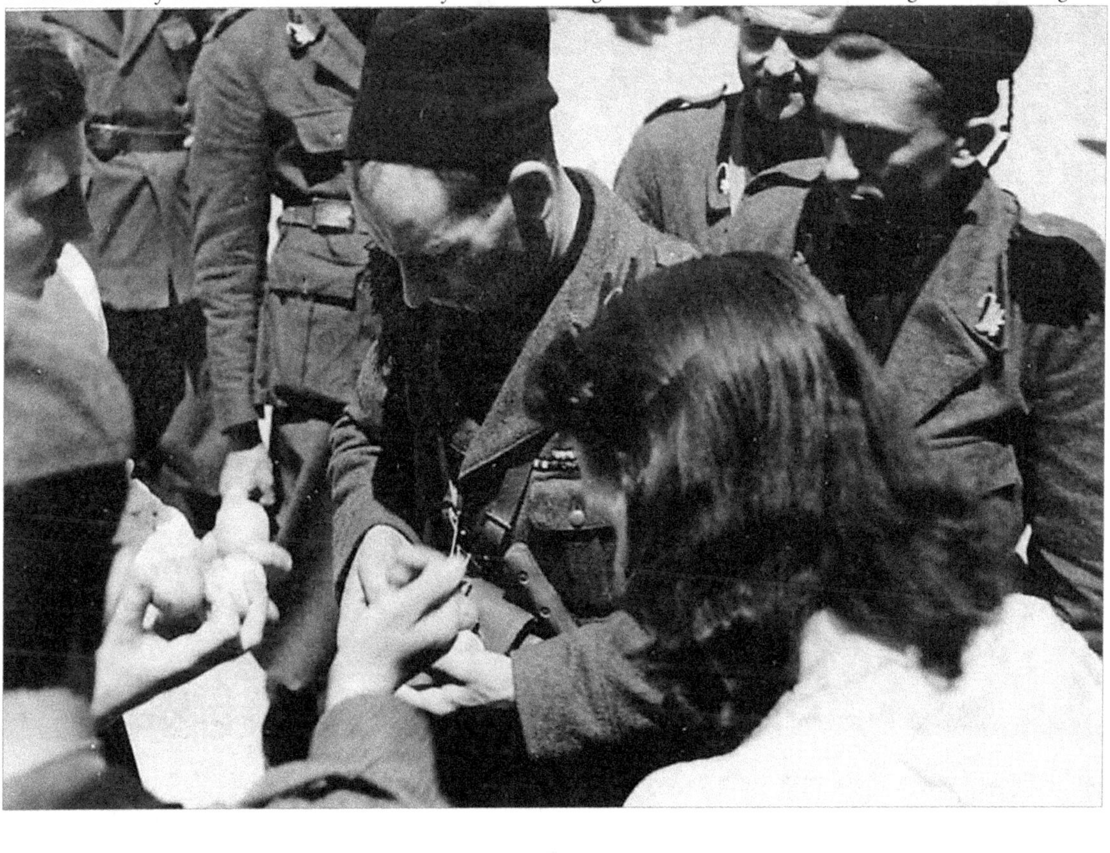

▲ The ruins of the city of Stalino destroyed by the fighting.

THE SECOND DEFENSIVE BATTLE OF THE DON AND THE WITHDRAWAL, DECEMBER 1942-JANUARY 1943

The Raggruppamento *3 Gennaio* was able to stand out in the fighting of December 1942, attempting to stop the Soviet offensive known as Little Saturn, which had overwhelmed the ARMIR.

The Black Shirts were involved in the tragedy of the retreat, opening the way several times in the Soviet barriers, and managing to re-enter the Axis deployment after being decimated. On December 16th, the Soviets of the 38th *Guards* attacked at six in the morning, without preparation of artillery or rocket launchers, but with a strong mortar fire all over the divisional front of the *Pasubio*, particularly in the Krasnogorowka-Abrossinowo- Monastyrschina stretch.

Defensive positions were invested, and above all the strongpoint *Olimpo* (Olympus) held by the 1st Battalion of the 79th infantry Regiment. For this reason the command of the *Pasubio* Division ordered the *Tagliamento* Group to intervene in aid of the infantrymen.

While the order was being executed, and the LXIII Battalion M hurried to reach *Olimpo*, the strongpoint
fell into Soviet hands, and given the situation the companies of Black Shirts were employed to regain possession of them as they arrived on the field, inorganically, since there was no time to assemble the Battalion; but if on the one hand this allowed the prompt use and the introduction of fresh forces, on the other it lacked organicity and dispersed the impact force of the LXIII M in a series of weak marks rather than using the force of the mass.

At 11.30, given the impossibility of stopping the enemy, the commander of the 1st Battalion of the 79th ordered the disengagement of the now-mixed departments of infantrymen and legionnaires and the folding on the positions of altitude 201, where it was believed that German departments of the *InfRgt* 520. of the 298.*Infanterie-Division*.

At the time of the release order, the LXIII Battalion M could only have 163 men.

The retreat on quote 201 caused a contraction in the size of the deployment, but despite the improvement of the defensive situation that had occurred, it was also necessary to insert the other Battalion of the *Tagliamento*, the LXXIX Battalion M, which, recalled by Getreide, arrived around at 13.00 siding between the remains of the LXIII ° M and the VI ° M of the *Montebello* Group also bleeding in the fights sustained during the day at the Artykulnyj Schlucht valley.

Meanwhile, Consul Galardo had replaced the First Seniore Rosmino as commander of the *Tagliamento* Group (Rosmino had been interim commander in the previous days) and it was precisely to Galardo that in the evening he was entrusted with the command of the sector, instead of Colonel Mazzocchi, commander of the 79 Rome Regiment.

On the morning of December 17th the Soviets attacked the Italian-Germans (as mentioned there were departments of 520.), trying to break through on altitude 201, since possession of this, halfway through the defensive line, would have allowed to reach Getreide and Malewany encircling *Pasubio*.

Incredibly given the situation, in spite of the reduced reaction of *Landser* and infantrymen, the Black Shirts managed to resist, but they went on the counterattack with the now consolidated tactics of throwing hand grenades to daze and frighten the opponents, putting the *Guards* on the run and by moving the Italian-German defensive line forward one kilometer.

The Soviets reacted with a violent shooting of artillery and Katjusha and Vanjusha multiple rocket launchers, but the artillery intervened with counterbattery shots that had the not indifferent result of raising the morale of the defenders, who continued to fight and to repel opposing offensive bets for all day of eighteen; on the nineteenth, Vatutin's troops, given the uselessness of the attacks in the sector, slowed down operations, which instead flared up in the sector of the Italian Army Corps.

It was precisely on December 1942 that the documentable news about the Assault Group *Tagliamento* are lost.

Remember how sixteen, at the time of folding from the strongpoint *Olimpo* on the 201 altitude, 163 men remained among officers and Black Shirts.

It is probable that the few remains of the Group, deployed together with the 1st Battalion of the 79th infantry, and often mixed with the infantrymen, followed the fate of the *Pasubio*; in fact the unit commanded by Colonel Mazzocchi during the retreat, carried out together with the remains of the Sforzesca, bore the name of Mazzocchi training Regiment, and not of 79th *Roma* infantry Regiment, indicative of the presence of other departments, including probably what remained of the *Tagliamento* group.

The retreat ended eleven days later in Morosowskaja, where the Mazzocchi column arrived on January 30th, after having traveled a long and tortuous path behind Vatutin's units advancing towards the Donetz basin.

he VI Battalion CC.NN. M on the morning of 11 December was, as mentioned, in Poltawka, where he received the order to move to Getreide to make himself available to the command of the *Pasubio* Division, what was carried out by fourteen.

At 1.30 on 12th December, the *Pasubio* commander, general Guido Boselli ordered Consul Goldoni to move with the 6th Battalion M on the *Olimpo* stronghold, placing himself at the disposal of the col. Mazzocchi; shortly after the order was modified, and the 6th would have had to reach the stronghold X instead, placing itself under the control of the *Tagliamento* Group bled in the fighting in Ogalew against the 38th riflemen Division of the *Guards*. At seven the legionnaires of the VIth reached the comrades who were engaged by the enemy.

At nine the 6th M Battalion moved on the counterattack in the Ogalew sector, as previously mentioned, and after two hours of hand-to-hand combat with hand grenades and daggers the Soviet riflemen retreated, leaving two hundred dead on the ground, chased by the legionaries so much that some Black Shirts, in the heat of pursuit, crossed the Don gelato arriving on the right bank.

Several prisoners and weapons were also taken, including some PTRD anti-tank rifles that proved very useful during the retreat.

The *Montebello* Group's Black Shirts had reported the following losses until then: 17 dead (3 officers), 78 injured (5 officers), 24 seriously frozen

The next day the Soviets, even without carrying out infantry actions, repeatedly bombed the town of Ogalew, or rather what was left of it, with rocket launches, artillery shells and heavy mortars.

In the evening the infantry destroyers of the fifteenth Battalion changed the Black Shirts, and on the fourteenth morning the legionaries of the sixth Battalion M reached the positions of Getreide.

▲ Polish Jews in charge of transport and cleaning a station in the summer of 1942.

▼ Russian girls in a station play with black shirts, the 'fascist enemy' of Stalinist propaganda.

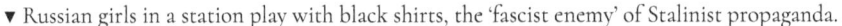

▲ Battalion "M" truck marching in the summer of 1942.

▼ The M battalions of the Lioness Group arrive in Russia.

In the night between 15th and 16th December, the *Montebello* Group was placed under the tactical dependence of the 80th *Roma* Regiment, attacked by the enemy, and at five in the morning the transfer began to the Artykulnyj Schlucht area.

The 80th infantry was withdrawing under pressure from the Soviet riflemen, who overwhelmed the pieces of the 201st Artillery Regiment: the servants of a battery, faithful to the motto of the Italian Artillery with this or above it, they were massacred to the last man on their 47/32 guns.

The enemy action developed with particular vigor on the Krasnogorowka-Abrossimowo-Monastyrschina line, with the support of mortars.

The Black Shirts launched into the reconquest of the 175.5, 178.3 and 187.6 hills, overlying the valley of Artykulnyj Schlucht, on which the Soviets were attesting after having routed the Italian infantrymen, and from which they could have reached Getreide by cutting off all the troops present in the area.

The three odds were taken after the assault by the legionaries and the *Guards* fell back.

General Boselli therefore ordered that the *Montebello* Group position itself from the south-western offshoots of altitude 201 until it overlooks the Monastyrschina-Getreide valley, between the LXXIX° M Battalion of the *Tagliamento* Group on the left and a small stronghold held by infantrymen of the 80th *Roma* on the left; the line was totally devoid of defensive works and the frozen ground (as mentioned, -35° during the day) did not allow excavation of posts or trenches.

After the fighting of Artykulnyj Schlucht the casualties had risen to 53 dead (4 officers), 117 injured (7 officers) and 27 serious frozen (2 officers), which added to those of the days from

▲ Battalion "M" truck marching in the summer of 1942.

December 10 to December 12 rose to 446 units, that is fifty percent of the fighting force.
On the seventeen the Soviets resumed the attacks contained by the Italian artillery; throughout the day attacks and counterattacks were repeated which cost the two contenders serious losses of personnel and materials.
But in addition to the enemy, the legionaries had to fight with another enemy, the cold.
In the night on the 18th, the very low temperature caused new victims.

The legionnaires of the VIth M, as Piero Calamai, at time a very young volounteer, recalls, were wrapped in "three quarters" coats because the fur coats remained in Verona. They always wore the helmet on the head wrapped in blankets, because the balaclavas had remained in Verona, along with the gloves. They had double-folded clothes pegs to keep warm and long-haired beards. They held their arms with their bare hands, but trying not to touch the iron with their hands so as not to leave the skin attached.

Generals Lucas and De Vecchi, in turn, remembered the stoicism of the frozen legionnaires, who wanted to return to their combat post after the brief treatments received at the dressing posts, realizing that only in this way could they prevent the thin defensive veil still in able to resist weakened more.
Worse, the enemy patrols, well camouflaged in the padded camouflage suits, infiltrated the Italian lines, and against which, formed by elite troops, little could collect the items collected, the result of scraping the barrel, sent against them, like a Battalion of Railway Engineers, certainly not trained to clash with selected troops.
At dawn on the 18th the *Guards* launched new violent attacks, including one against quota 201.1 held by the Black Shirts of the Grouping *January 3*, by a few infantrymen of the *Pasubio* and by the Germans of 520./298., Which was rejected in practice only by the Black Shirts and Italian artillery, inflicting heavy losses on the enemy; the artillery had also hit some Soviet batteries in full that were supposed to support the attack with their shot.
In the afternoon, Italian patrols came out of the Italian lines in order to ascertain the situation, which provoked the opposing reaction and hard clashes. As darkness fell the patrols returned after taking prisoners and materials.
The increasingly degraded situation led General Zingales, commander of the XXXV Corps, to personally order the commander of *Pasubio* Boselli to withdraw.
At 3 pm the advance notice of movement arrived to reach the backward Werchnje Miskowici-Nasarow line; the *3 Gennaio* Battlegroup, or rather, the *Montebello* Group, would have been among the rear departments.
At night the village of Medowa was reached; the retreat resumed and at nine o'clock on 20 December it reached Popowka.
But the Soviets had surrounded the retreating departments: Black Shirts, Germans and infantrymen of the *Torino* managed to break the enemy circle, and the XXXV Corps continued the retreat, increasingly thinned by the losses due also to the air attacks.
At 10 pm the column arrived in Posdnjakow, where the departments stayed until the morning of the next day, when the retreat was resumed.
On 22nd Soviet units had blocked the way to the columns in retreat in Arbusow: once again it was the Black Shirts that opened the way, thanks also to the sacrifice of the Battle Assistant

▲ A truck of the CCNN Grouping 'March 23' in Russia, summer 1942.

▲ Ukrainian women watch the black shirt trucks.

▼ M Battalions enter a village, Russia 1942.

Biagi, who placed himself at the head of his men breaking through the enemy lines , and earning the Golden Medal for Military Valor.

The remains of the M battalions had managed to break through, attacking the Soviets, but with heavy losses: the *Montebello* Group alone had had 115 dead, 380 wounded, 66 frozen in action; among the losses thirty-two are officers.

The Seniors Goldoni and Superti had fallen leading in battle their men.

At 11 pm the column started moving again; only the most valuable elements could follow her, injured and frozen were left on the spot, later being massacred by the Stalinist troops.

The cohesion of the units, even of the veteran ones, was flaking, many threw down their arms to try to lighten themselves; in the mounting chaos the remains of the M battalions were among the few to maintain an organic structure.

At nine o'clock on December 24th, the column, better, what remained of it reached Bukarewskij, and at sunset it reached Pressiannowskji; on Christmas Eve the Italians continued to retire until they reached ten in the morning of 25th in Scheptukowa.

The pause lasted only four hours, because the pressing of the Soviet armored units was pressing, and the march had already started again at fourteen.

At one o'clock on the morning of 26th December, the survivors arrived in Tcherkowo, standing in defense in the town where the remains of the column of the II Army Corps were already located.

Soviets locked below, and began a siege destined to last twenty days.

The XXXV ° Corps, with the remains of *Pasubio*, *Torino* and *Ravenna* Divisions, of the 298. InfDiv., of the *3 Gennaio* Group and remains of *Roman*ian units contributed to the defense of Tcherkowo in training units.

The *Montebello* Group was now unable to line up more than two hundred men capable of fighting, but the Black Shirts sacrificed themselves on January 9th, 1943 to stop a violent Soviet attack, preceded by a strong preparatory bombing and supported by nine T34 tanks .

When the T34s and the infantry carried by them shouting *Hurrà* Stalin arrived, the legionnaires responded by intoning Youth and aiming with automatic weapons at the infantry transported by the wagons before they could set foot on the ground.

A T34 was set on fire by the Black Shirt Gino Betti, who arrested him with a shot of a PTRD anti-tank shotgun of war, after waiting with great cold blood for the wagon to arrive just ten meters from its position.

To every chariot hit the legionaries shouted *Viva il Duce!* and they sang the Fascist anthem *Giovinezza.*

The head injured Lamberto Vannutelli, already wounded, had been crushed by a Soviet tank, but found the strength to intone *Giovinezza* when the T34 was hit by his men.

In the counterattacks, fell the twice wounded leutnant (capomanipolo)Cremisi , who, having exhausted his ammunition, swirled the musket like a club against the Soviets that surrounded him. His heroism earned him the Golden Medal in memory.

The second Golden Medal awardedof the day also fell in battle, the Black Shirt Gianfilippo Braccini, already decorated on the field for the fighting of the previous days, who, wounded twice, did not want to receive help, continuing to shoot with his submachine gun, was hit when to better aim, he had moved to a better position from which he fired on the attackers.

The Black Shirt Stefano Migliavacca, frozen on his feet, replied to his officer that he wanted to force him to stay in the dressing place that to shoot with the machine gun it was not necessary to march; having vainly seen his protests, he had the comrades secretly take him to a very exposed position, and remained there for forty-eight hours, despite a new wound from a sliver of grenade, keeping the Soviets under fire with his own weapon.

In two hours of struggle sixty Black Shirts destroyed eight wagons out of nine and completely destroyed the Soviet Battalion, losing two fallen (1 officers), 11 wounded (2 officers) and 17 frozen.

The admired German captain Lewandosky proposed to the command of the 298. Infanteriedivision all the Black Shirts present for the 2nd Class Iron Cross.

Finally on January 15th the remains of the 298. Infanteriedivision and the three hundred surviving Black Shirts of the *Montebello* Group managed to break the encirclement and open a way to Losowskaja.

The Italians only had two trucks and some sleds that were used to evacuate the most seriously injured, but if 2800 wounded able to walk, several hundred serious and frozen injured joined the column had to be abandoned to their fate.

Between 16th and 17th January the remains of the XXXV and II Army Corps reached Belowdosk. When on 30th December the Army Command ordered the formation of two battalions with the remains of the Battlegroups *3 Gennaio* and *23 Marzo*, the formation of the one based on the *3 Gennaio* had to be postponed, due to the state in which the survivors were reduced,

▲ M truck battalions in transfer in the summer of 1942.

When the new commander, Consul Alessandro Lusana, received the order from the Chief of Staff of the XXXV Corps, Colonel Vargas, at the command of the Grouping, who at the beginning of the retreat was in Malewanyi at the command of the *Pasubio* to reach the base of the Grouping already started towards Tcherkowo.

The presence of Soviet armored vehicles infiltrating the roads leading to Tcherkowo led the Consul Lusana to go to Millerovo with the group command and with the vehicles gathered along the way.

When he arrived in Millerovo, he informed the Army Command of the situation, and arranged to gather about four thousand soldiers of the various armed forces in training units, despite the difficulties caused by the activity of the Soviet aviation, now master of the skies.

The training troops moved to Woroshilowgrad on the night of December 20-21, while the Group Command remained in Millerovo, which was however isolated from an armored brigade of the 25th Armored Corps of the *Guards*.

During his stay in the town, the Command managed to organize a radio interception service for opposing communications, which proved to be very useful in defending the town.

The Command of 3 *Gennaio* remained in the town until January 7th, 1943, when he received authorization to leave Millerovo and move to Woroshilowgrad, which he did by joining German 298. InfDiv on a sortie that managed to break the Soviet circle.

At the end of the retreat, the 3 January Grouping had suffered 2170 losses, equal to 77.5 percent of the workforce on 1st December 1942.

When it was decided to create two companies (!) With the remains of the two groupings, only the one with the veterans of 23 Marzo could be formed. The 3 *Gennaio* he had been too tried to put together any unit.

"When we left Italy in August 1941, we were in 1613. After the battles of the first winter, we stayed in 654.

The Legion had therefore lost 959 staff. Transformed into a group, the "Tagliamento" recorded losses recorded in 458 men in the battles of August '42. Then the furnace of the "Berretto Frigio" (Don's handle) came on; the grueling days of the retreat came, and 1061 other legionaries did not respond to the appeal. When on March 25, 1943, the Tagliamento's labaro decorated with a golden medal for military valor, he left the field in Bologna to be returned to the Shrine of Udine, 153 legionnaires escorted him. The 2478 missing were only a memory preserved in the heart of the small handful of survivors".

▲ ARMIR vehicles in the Donetz basin.

▼ The CCNN column crosses Ukrainian civilians moving away from the front line.

▲ Near the front, continue on foot.

▼ Grouping XXIII March soldiers marching into a Russian village.

▲ Communist symbols are destroyed. Note on the hammer the Cyrillic writing *Lenin kaputt*.

▼ Francisci gives a speech at the Grouping March 23, USSR 1942.

▲ Francisci speaks to CCNN 'M' Grouping March 23.

▼ Russia. General Enrico Francisci spoke to the 15th M battalion the day before his departure to the front lines in the summer of 1942.

▲ The Grouping March 23 deployed.

▼ Francisci reviews the Grouping 23 March.

▲ Legionnaires in the USSR, summer 1942.

▼ Soviet prisoners captured by Black Shirts.

▲ Column of Russian prisoners in the summer of 1942.

▼ A bridge destroyed over the Donez in Ukraine in the summer of 1942.

▲ Lieutenant General Enrico Francisci with the officers of the Group CC.NN. "March 23" and German military authorities.

▼ General Enrico Francisci with Italian and German officers on the same occasion.

▲ Enrico Francisci with the officers of the CCNN Group 'March 23' and German and Italian military authorities pay homage to the German fallen in a Germanic war cemetery.

▼ Francisci with the officers of the regr. 23 March pays tribute to the fallen Germans.

THE MVSN CROATIAN LEGION (HRVATSKE LEGIJA)

After the conquest of Yugoslavia and the creation of the kingdom of Croatia (of which Aimone of Savoy Aosta was proclaimed King with the name of Tomislav III) the poglavnik Ante Pavelich decided to support the Axis war operations, creating a Croatian legion, also supported by an air force, which would flank the Germans on the Soviet front.

Later, towards the end of 1941, the creation of a similar unit (but without air component) was ordered to fight alongside the Italians on the Russian front, also to give a sign of goodwill to Italy, which had with the new Croatian state causes tension for Dalmatia.

To try to ease the tensions that arose between Italy and Croatia, Pavelich consented to the creation of a voluntary Legion under Italian command.

For political reasons, the unit, made up of two infantry battalions and one accompanying weapons, framing 1,211 men, was placed under the National Security Voluntary Militia with regard to classification, weapons and equipment.

The Croatian Legion (Hrvatske Legija) wore the Italian 1940 model uniform with black flames and the Militia fasci on the lapel.

On the right arm of the jacket and coat was sewn the coat of arms of Croatia, with the word Hrvatska on the red white chessboard.

The Croatian legionaries wore the black shirt but not the fez, replaced by the Italian service cap (bustina) with the frieze of the M.V.S.N.

The Legion was formed in Varazdin, near the Hungarian border, and also included Ustasha officers who spoke Italian, having lived in Italy as escaped.

The first employment of the legionnairies was against Tito's communist partisans; the Legion was then moved to Italy, in Riva del Garda, where the depot was located, to further train and assimilate Italian combat tactics. Here the legionnairies swore allegiance to the Duce and the poglavnik Pavelich, and in March '41 the trains carrying the Croats left in staggering for the Soviet front.

Arriving in Ukraine, the departments gathered on April 16th, receiving numerous vehicles, and being joined to the 63rd *Tagliamento* Legion in Wladimirowka.

However, several problems arose which advised against the continued use of Slavic legionaries on line.

After a reorganization and the anti-partisan use in the rear, conducted with the imaginable Balkan hardness, the Croatian Legion returned to the frontline in July, behaving this time well, so much so that the Legion had several rewards and numerous losses.

The Soviets, in fact, killed all the Croatian prisoners on the spot, both because they were fascists and because they were considered traitors of their Yugoslav ally.

At the beginning of the offensive on Krasnij Lutsch, on the morning of 11th July 1941, the Croatian Black Shirts attacked the 253.4 share of Vessielj, held by elements of the 216th Soviet Division, managing to seize it. The flag of the Croatian contingent was personally decorated by General Gariboldi, commander of ARM.I.R.

The Croatian Legion worked together with the Battalions Group CC.NN. M *Tagliamento* in the sector of Schterowka and Surajewka, and together with the *Tagliamento* and the 3rd group of the Horse Artillery Regiment the Legion was part of the Mittica Group, which chased the Soviets towards Krasnaja Poliana during the maneuver of Krasnij Lutsch. The Croatian legionnaires fought first in Kolpakowo and Krasnaja Poliana on the afternoon of July 18th.

The Legion was then incorporated in the Raggruppamento *3 Gennaio*, and continued to operate in a very satisfactory way, without this time any friction between Croatians and Italians arose. The Croats fought, together with the *Pasubio* Division, to which it had been placed, in the first defensive battle of the Don in August 1942.

In December, Croatian volunteers were overwhelmed by the Soviet offensive Malyï Saturn and withdrew with the remains of the ARM.IR, but during the retreat, the Legion lost almost all its men between fallen and missing (to be considered dead) in the clashes at the village of Kasanskaya. Concluding the report on the operating cycle of December 17-21, the command of the Celere Division wrote:

Not a man from the 3rd Bersaglieri regt. went back. Of the Croatian legion: an officer and a soldier survive.

In 1943 new Croatian volunteers flocked to Riva del Garda to replenish the Legion; after September 8th, the volunteers were repatriated and placed in the Divisions 373. and 392. of the Nezavisna Drzava Hrvatska, the Croatian Independent State, placed in the Wehrmacht.

▲ German soldiers examine a destroyed Katiusha.

▲ Soviet counterattack in the Voronez sector.

▼ The Chief of Staff of MVSN Galbiati with the Labar of the Tagliamento Legion, Russian front 1942.

▲ Galbiati with the 8th Army Chief of Staff, General B. Malaguti, in conversation with Consul General I. Vianini and other senior officers of the Militia on the Eastern Front.

▼ Legionaries of the Tagliamento Group, Russian front summer 1942.

▲ Black Shirts of the Tagliamento Group, Russian front summer 1942.

▼ Soviet civilians (or deserters...) interrogated by the Black Shirts.

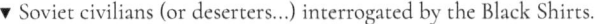

▲ The tomb of a fallen centurion. His legionnaires nailed a red "M" of enamel to the cross.

▼ The 'M' legionnaires amass straw for the winter quarters.

▲ Legionnaire 'M' on the front line on the Don.

▼ Black Shirts in Russia. Winter is coming.

▲ Position of the 15th CC.NN. machine gun company in the snow, winter 1942.

▼ A Militia Breda in action. Winter 1942.

▲ Reggio Emilia, March 1943. Show organized by the 35 infantry in honour of the veterans of the '23 March' group.

▼ The labaro of the 63rd Tagliamento Legion, decorated with Golden and Silver Medals for Military Valor - The motivation of the Gold one states:Heir and continuator of Black Shirtsíunits. of which, with the name, it assumed titles of reputation and value, during the pursuit of a fierce and expert enemy, it reaffirmed combative temper, secure prowess and military solidity. Dislocated in a flanking position in a sector of delicate importance, at the first alarm, it leapt compactly against Bolshevik columns, which tried to gain ground on the right of the Don, and in bloody duels, it curbed its impact. Subsequently surrounded in a stronghold, it resisted it intrepid for many days, enduring serious losses in deaths and injuries. As the ammunition was about to run out, the survivors made their way through the enemies with hand grenades: they broke the blockade and reached other positions with nearby fighters with unaltered offensive spirit and indomitable will to recover.

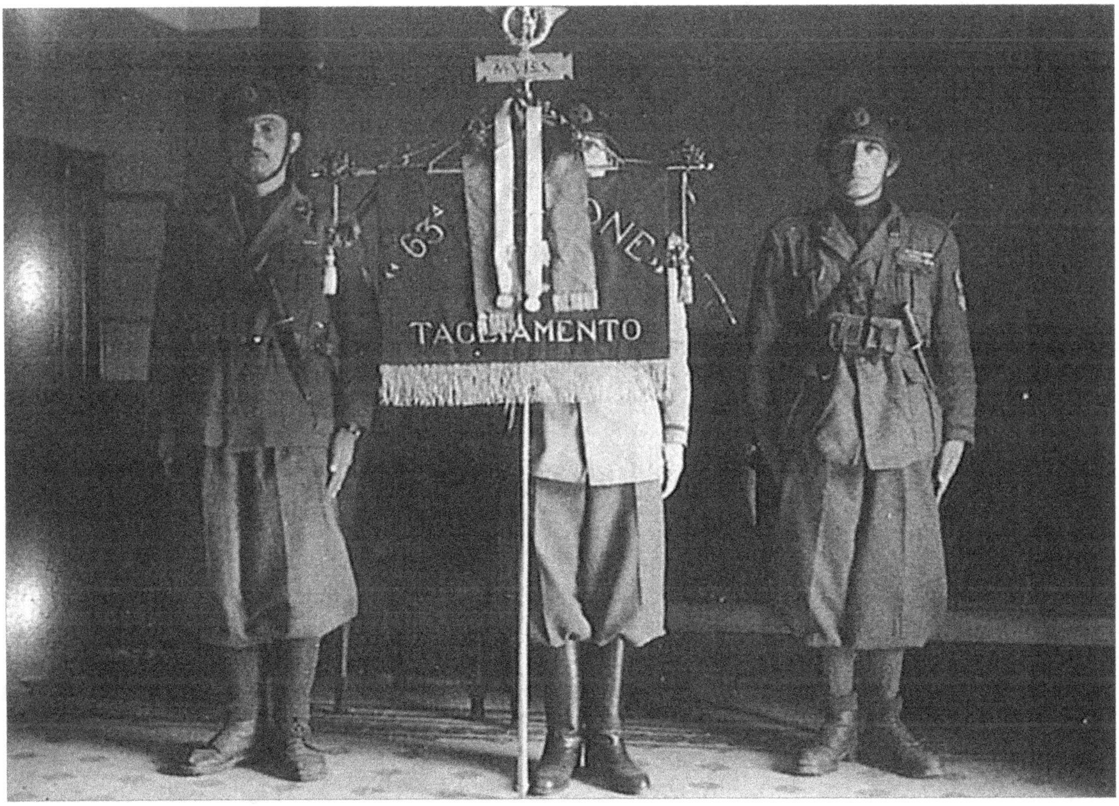

▲ Russian front badge.

▼ CSIR in Russia.

▲ Second defensive battle of the Don.

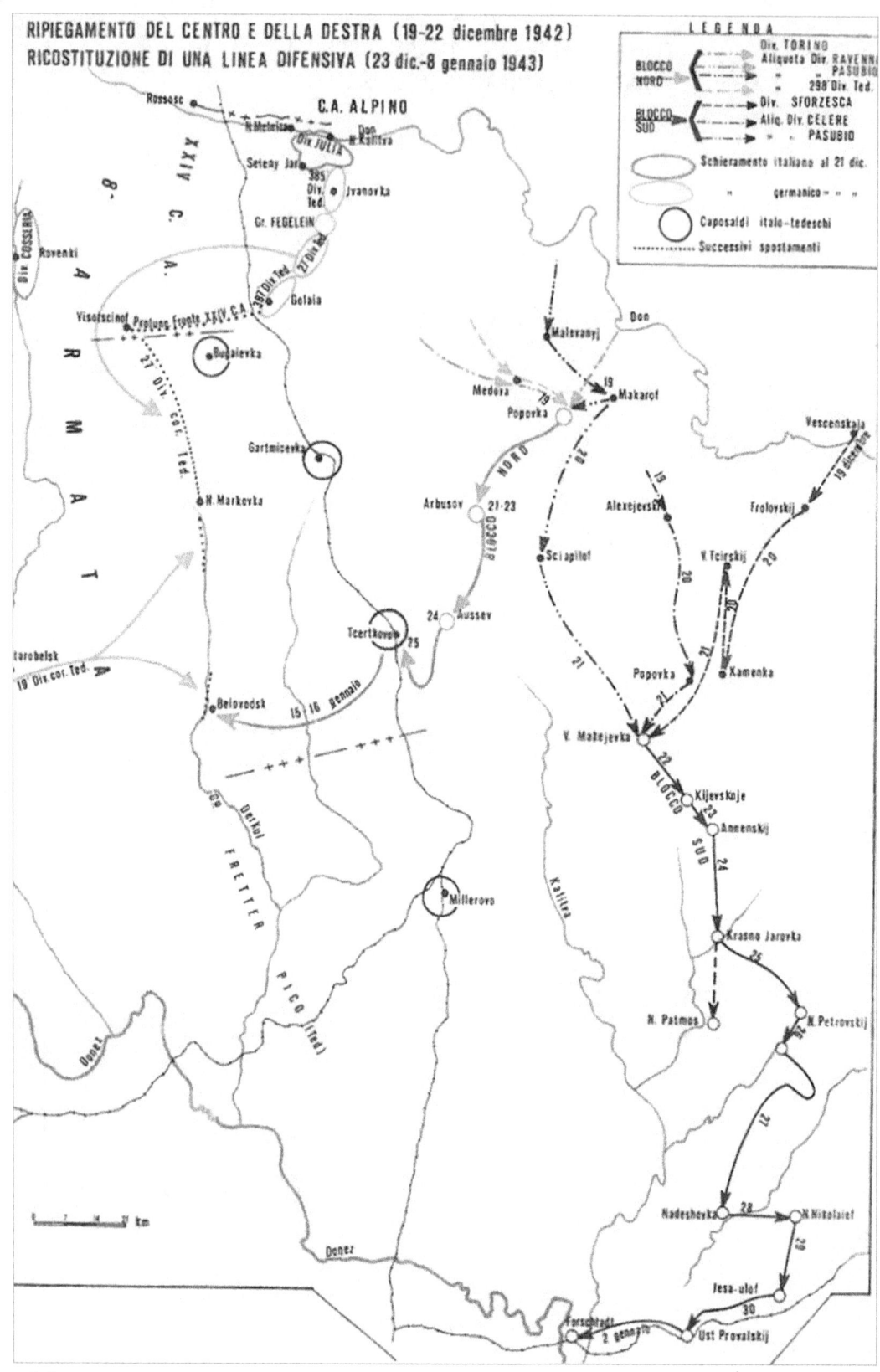
▲ Italian retreat 1942-43.

▲ The airport of Stalino conquered by the Black Shirts.

▼ Machine gunners from the "Tagliamento" in Orlowka, December 1941.

BIBLIOGRAPHY

AAVV 1962, *Milizia Armata di Popolo*, Roma.

O. Bovio 1999, *In alto la bandiera. Storia del Regio Esercito*, Foggia

P. Cappellari 2013, *La Guardia della Rivoluzione. La Milizia fascista nel 1943: crisi militare – 25 Luglio – 8 Settembre – Repubblica Sociale*, Roma

E. Galbiati 1942, *Battaglioni M*, Roma.

S. Jowett 2000, *The Italian Army 1940- 1945 [1] Europe 1940-43*, Oxford.

L. Lenzi 1968, *Dal Dnjeper al Don. Storia della 63ª Legione CC.NN. Tagliamento nella campagna di Russia*, Roma.

E. Lucas, G. De Vecchi 1976, *Storia delle unità combattenti della M.V.S.N.*, Roma.

L. Malatesta 2015, *Storia della Legione Tagliamento. Dalla guerra di Russia all'Armistizio*, Varese

G. Messe 1963, *La guerra al fronte russo. Il Corpo di Spedizione Italiano in Russia (C.S.I.R.)*, Vª ed, Milano.

A Mollo 1981, *The Armed Forces of World War II*, London (tr. it. Novara 1982).

C. Rastrelli 2016, *L'ultimo comandande delle camicie nere: Enzo Emilio Galbiati*, Milano.

O. Ricchi, L. Striuli 2007, *Fronte Russo. C.S.I.R. Operations 1941- 1942*, Virginia Beach.

P. Romeo di Colloredo 2008, *Emme rossa! Le Camicie Nere in Russia 1941- 1943*, Genova.

P. Romeo di Colloredo 2009, *I Pretoriani di Mussolini. Storia militare della Milizia Volontaria per la Sicurezza Nazionale*, Roma.

P. Romeo di Colloredo 2010, *Croce di ghiaccio. CSIR e ARMIR in Russia*, Genova.

P. Romeo di Colloredo 2010, *Talianskij karashoi. La Campagna di Russia tra mito e rimozione*, Genova.

P. Romeo di Colloredo 2018, *Camicia Nera! Storia delle unità combattenti della Milizia Volontaria Sicurezza Nazionale dalle origini al 25 luglio*, Bergamo

P. Romeo di Colloredo 2019, *Per vincere ci vogliono i leoni… I fronti dimenticati delle camicie nere, 1939- 1940*, Bergamo

G. Rosignoli 1995, *M.V.S.N.. Storia, organizzazione, uniformi e distintivi*, Parma.

G. Rochat 2006, *Le guerre italiane 1935-1943. Dall'impero d'Etiopia alla disfatta*, Torino.

A. Rossi 2004, *La guerra delle camicie nere. La milizia fascista dalla Guerra mondiale alla guerra civile*, Pisa.

Ufficio Storico dello Stato Maggiore dell'Esercito 1946, *L'8ª Armata italiana nella Seconda battaglia difensiva del Don (11 gennaio 1942- 31 gennaio 1943)*, Roma.

Ufficio Storico dello Stato Maggiore dell'Esercito 1948, *Le operazioni del C.S.I.R. e dell'Armir dal giugno 1941 all'ottobre 1942*, Roma.

Ufficio Storico dello Stato Maggiore dell'Esercito 2000, *Le operazioni delle Unità italiane al Fronte russo*, IVª ed, Roma.

F. Valori 1967, *Gli italiani in Russia. La Campagna del C.S.I.R. e dell'ARMIR*, Milano.

P. Zanlucchi 2014, *La milizia del Duce muore sul Don: la 41 a Legione Cesare Battisti: memorie dal fronte russo 1942- 43*, Rovereto, 2014

TITLES ALREADY PUBLISHED

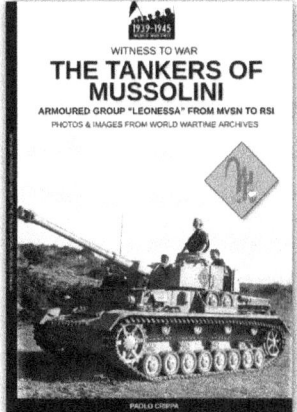

www.ingramcontent.com/pod-product-compliance
Lightning Source LLC
LaVergne TN
LVHW081544070526
838199LV00057B/3772